THE AMERICAN CIVIL WAR

★ THE RIGHT ANSWER ★

AFTER THE WAR

Tim Cooke

Gareth Stevens
Publishing

Please visit our website, www.garethstevens.com. For a free color catalog of all our high-quality books, call toll free 1-800-542-2595 or fax 1-877-542-2596.

Library of Congress Cataloging-in-Publication Data

Cooke, Tim, 1961-
 After the war / Tim Cooke.
     p. cm. — (The American Civil War : the right answer)
 Includes index.
ISBN 978-1-4339-7532-5 (pbk.)
ISBN 978-1-4339-7533-2 (6-pack)
ISBN 978-1-4339-7531-8 (library binding)
1. United States—History—1865-1898—Juvenile literature. 2. United States—History—
Civil War, 1861-1865—Influence—Juvenile literature. 3. Reconstruction (U.S. history,
1865-1877)—Juvenile literature. I. Title.
  E661.C76 2013
  973.7—dc23

                                        2012012858

Published in 2013 by
Gareth Stevens Publishing
111 East 14th Street, Suite 349
New York, NY 10003

© 2013 Brown Bear Books Ltd.

For Brown Bear Books Ltd:
Editorial Director: Lindsey Lowe
Managing Editor: Tim Cooke
Children's Publisher: Anne O'Daly
Art Director: Jeni Child
Designer: Karen Perry
Picture Manager: Sophie Mortimer
Production Director: Alastair Gourlay

Picture Credits
Front Cover: Getty Images

Interior: all Library of Congress except, Corbis: 18, 36, Bettmann 34, 35; National
Archives: 11, 24; Photodisc: 40, R Morley 20;Robert Hunt Library: 21; Thinkstock:
Comstock 5, istockphoto 19, 29, 41.

All Artworks © Brown Bear Books Ltd.

Manufactured in the United States of America
1 2 3 4 5 6 7 8 9   12 11 10

CPSIA compliance information: Batch #BRS11GS: For further information contact Gareth Stevens, New York, New York
at 1-800-542-2595.

Contents

Introduction

The Civil War ended about 150 years ago. But its legacy continues to shape life in the United States. And it remains a constant presence in American culture, from books to movies.

For those people who stood to benefit most from the Union victory, the outcome of the war could be disappointing. Millions of liberated slaves found themselves without work or forced to work for their former masters in jobs that resembled the conditions of slavery. During Reconstruction (1865–1877), the federal government used U.S. troops to enforce the rights of African Americans. The experiment eventually failed, however, due to Southern resistance and corruption and lack of commitment in the North. By 1900, conditions for black Americans were as bad as at any time since the end of the war.

Cultural impact

Meanwhile, Americans were still becoming accustomed to the fact that the war had even happened. On both sides, people developed a series of ceremonies and memorials that honored the memory of the dead. Such shared observances helped achieve a certain amount of reconciliation, despite the insistence of some

Southerners that their cause had been right along; the Union had simply misunderstood the Southern way of life. Soon, too, the drama and upheaval of the war began to attract poets and novelists and, with the invention of the movies a generation after the war's end, filmmakers, too.

About this book

This book describes the war's aftermath and its lasting impact. Boxes in the margins help you get more out of your reading. **Comment** boxes highlight specific information and explain its importance. **Ask Yourself** boxes suggest questions for you to consider. There are no right or wrong answers; the questions are meant to help you think about the subject. Other boxes explain difficult words or ideas. The book finishes with a glossary and a list of resources for further information. There is also an index that you can use to find facts fast.

↻ For some people, the Civil War remains alive through reenactments, like the raising of the Confederate flag in this mock battle.

Carpetbaggers and Scalawags

Supporters of the Republican Party in the South were singled out for criticism by Southerners.

The immediate postwar period is known as Reconstruction (1865–1877). The Republican Party, which was already dominant in the North, now became dominant in the South, too. By 1870, all the former Confederate states had rejoined the Union, and the Republicans controlled most of them. Much Republican support came from former slaves, who now had the vote for the first time.

🎧 *"The murder of Louisiana" is a cartoon about the election of William P. Kellogg as state governor in 1872. Many people thought his election had been fixed.*

Carpetbaggers and Scalawags

The terms "carpetbagger" and "scalawag" were made up by Democrats to criticize the Republicans. "Carpetbagger" was a term for an uneducated Northerner who moved South after the war to look for economic opportunities. "Scalawag" referred to native Southerners who became Republicans after the war.

Southern hostility

Many white Southerners hated the Republicans who controlled state governments. They resented tax raises they felt they could not afford. They resented the widespread corruption among officials. They disliked the carpetbaggers and scalawags who worked to improve the lives of freed slaves.

Carpetbaggers and scalawags divide opinion. The Southern view was that they were driven by greed and used black Americans for their own ends. But another view points out that many carpetbaggers came to the South genuinely seeking to help the former slaves. Some worked for the Freedmen's Bureau, a federal organization set up to help former slaves make the change to freedom. Many slaves were educated as lawyers and teachers; others hoped to start small businesses.

Many former Union soldiers moved South after the war. Of the 60 carpetbagger politicians who served in Congress, 52 had served in the Union armies.

> The term "carpetbagger" came from a large bag in which a poor man was said to be able to carry all his possessions. "Scalawag" was a word for a scoundrel.

↻ Adelbert Ames was a carpetbagger governor of Mississippi. His position was very controversial in a state that was one of the last to rejoin the Union.

Joining the party

White Southern scalawags joined the Republican Party for different reasons. Some wanted to make money. Others refused to join the Democrats after the war. Some had stayed pro-Union throughout the conflict, and a few had even fought on the Union side.

Scalawags tended to come from the poorer, more mountainous parts of their states. They believed the Democrats had favored the wealthier regions with plantations before the war. A few wealthy planters in Mississippi and Louisiana also became scalawags, however. They liked the Republicans' plans for economic expansion.

After the war, some Democrats favored the Republicans due to prewar disagreements in their own party.

Republicans take charge

After 1867, Republicans won election to hundreds of offices, partly because former Confederate leaders were still barred from either voting or holding office. The governors of Arkansas, Louisiana, Mississippi, South Carolina, Georgia, and Florida were all carpetbaggers, 60 of whom were also elected to Congress.

When the carpetbagger William P. Kellogg became governor of Louisiana in 1872, many believed the election was fixed. On September 4, 1874, armed Democrats marched on the state capitol. Kellogg fled, and President Ulysses S. Grant had to send 22 warships to restore peace.

◌ *William P. Kellogg fled the Louisiana state capitol when it was attacked by an angry mob.*

A mixed bag

As elected officials, some of the carpetbaggers and scalawags served with distinction; but others did not. Some were involved in corruption, which undermined trust in the Southern Republican governments. However, corruption was not confined to the South. It was also a big problem in both the North and the West throughout the Reconstruction period.

The postwar Republican state governments did introduce several important reforms, however. These included establishing a public school system and reforming the tax system and the judiciary in the South.

ASK YOURSELF

Why do you think there was so much corruption at this time? Might it have been connected with the Civil War?

THE RIGHT ANSWER

?

What role do you think the carpetbaggers and scalawags really played in Reconstruction?

Historians are divided about the intentions of the carpetbaggers and the scalawags. There were good and bad examples of both. The good ones genuinely wanted to help the South. Some had fought in the war and did not want sacrifices made by the soldiers to have been in vain. Some wanted to right injustices done to the slaves. Others saw Reconstruction as an opportunity to become a farmer or store owner, helping rebuild the infrastructure of the South. But there were undoubtedly also many unscrupulous men who saw only a chance to make quick money for themselves.

Freedmen

Freedom for all Southern slaves came in December 1865, with the Thirteenth Amendment. By that time, however, many thousands of slaves had already been freed: they were known as freedmen.

COMMENT

The proclamation exempted five Union slave states: Missouri, Kentucky, Tennessee, Maryland, and Delaware.

⟳ **Freedmen cross into Union-held territory in North Carolina.**

Moves toward freeing the slaves had begun during the Civil War, particularly with the Emancipation Proclamation. Coming into force on January 1, 1863, it freed all slaves in regions that were fighting against the United States. Freedom for all slaves now awaited only a Union victory.

Generations of African American slaves had looked forward to the day of liberation. They called it the "day of jubilee" and celebrated it with religious devotion. But liberation was not the same as equality: many white Americans continued to look down on African Americans.

A lack of policy

The North had no clear policy about what to do with former slaves as they were freed during the war, as long as they did not help the Southern economy. But Union generals often did not want to keep freed

● *African American children study outside their school in a freedmen's village in Arlington, Virginia.*

slaves with their armies. As the Union armies took control of Southern territories, army commanders introduced a contract labor system for freedmen. This often forced slaves to stay on their former masters' plantations—although in theory they were now to be paid for their labor.

An unclear act

The Confiscation Act of July 1862 said that any slave captured behind Union lines was to be set free. But the act did not guarantee the former slaves any civil rights. It even allowed freedmen to be transported to overseas colonies in Central America, Haiti, and the African state of Liberia. (The policy was abandoned after around 100 settlers died due to a mixture of corruption and mismanagment in a colony on the Ile-a-Vache near Haiti in 1862–1863.)

Some Union army commanders still refused to deal with the freedmen even after Lincoln's Emancipation Proclamation. Lincoln ordered that

Forcing slaves to work for a wage on their former masters' plantations was described by one abolitionist as a new form of slavery.

ASK YOURSELF

Do you think the Union government thought it could get rid of the slavery issue by sending slaves overseas?

🎧 *A convoy of freedmen and their families arrive in Baltimore, Maryland, in 1865.*

Among African Americans who were forced to work unwillingly for the Union war effort, about 1 in 4 died.

freedmen be allowed to cross into Union-held territory. From spring 1863, the Union government also made a determined effort to recruit African American troops. More than 180,000 blacks eventually served in the Union army, nearly all of them freedmen. Freedmen also worked as laborers for the Union war effort, either voluntarily or as forced labor.

Many of the freedmen lived in camps for contrabands, the name given to runaway slaves. Some camps were well run, but others lacked even basic facilities and soon became unpleasant to live in. As well as terrible conditions and a lack of choice about what they did or where they went, freedmen also faced racism from Union soldiers. Many African American women were sexually abused by soldiers.

Central bureau

The problem of the freedmen continued, and the War Department finally set up the Freedmen's Bureau in March 1865. The new agency centralized help for former slaves. It handed out food and clothing, arranged education, and helped freedmen negotiate new labor contracts.

The Freedmen's Bureau lasted until 1872 and is widely seen as a failure. But for the former slaves, it was probably more helpful than not.

◯ *A freedman uses a primitive plow in South Carolina. Many freedmen lacked modern tools for farming.*

THE RIGHT ANSWER

?

Were the freedmen inevitable victims of the racism that existed in the United States?

At the start of the Civil War, Abraham Lincoln's government made it clear that ending slavery was not one of its war aims. That changed during the course of the war, however. The issue of slavery lay at the roots of the cause of the war, and Lincoln knew the issue had to be confronted once and for all. But many white Americans had been brought up to see African Americans as inferior. Even if the slaves were freed, they would still not be the equals of free whites. So it was in many ways inevitable that former slaves would face discrimination, even in the North.

Freedmen's Bureau

The Bureau of Refugees, Freedmen, and Abandoned Lands, better known as the Freedmen's Bureau, operated for seven years. It was one of the first federal social service agencies in the United States.

It took some two years of debate in Congress before the Freedmen's Bureau was set up on March 3, 1865. The new agency had various functions, principally dealing with newly freed slaves in the South.

A new bureau

The bureau was part of the U.S. War Department, and its head in Washington, D.C., was a soldier: Union general Oliver O. Howard. Howard had a network of local agents and commissioners in each state. In theory, the agents were backed by federal troops, but they often complained that such support was absent.

⊙ *An elderly African American reads a headline in his newspaper announcing the Emancipation Proclamation.*

The bureau was intended to raise money by selling confiscated land in the South. In fact, that land was restored to pardoned Confederates in 1866. The bureau lost its main source of money. Most freed slaves lost the chance to own land.

The bureau's work

The main work of the bureau's agents was to negotiate fair contracts on behalf of freedmen for labor agreements and property deals. Agents also set up churches and schools, built hospitals, and gave medical aid to more than a million freedmen. They distributed more than 21 million food rations to blacks and destitute whites, and helped reunite families divided by the war.

Education success

The bureau's greatest achievement came in education. It eastablished more than a thousand schools to teach black families to read and write. African American groups and Northern aid societies helped to build and equip the schools

ASK YOURSELF

Might the bureau have made people cross because it was part of the federal government but actually spent a lot of its time checking up on local government?

↻ *An illustration by Alfred Waud from 1868. A bureau agent stands between armed groups of white and black Southerners.*

and train and pay for teachers. Many white Southerners opposed educating blacks. They harassed teachers and burned down schools.

The historically black colleges that still exist today were established or funded by the bureau. They included Howard University in Washington, D.C., which was set up in March 1866.

Failings of the bureau

Most historians agree that, despite its idealism, the Freedmen's Bureau only had a limited effect. Its officials struggled to gain fair labor contracts for blacks. Most whites were still unwilling to treat African Americans as equals. The bureau and its agents did not seem to appreciate the deep divisions and distrust that still split the South between whites and blacks and between the wealthy and the poor.

Colleges for African Americans were founded to train black teachers and preachers to teach the next generation of black Americans.

⟲ *A lithograph shows a freedmen's school on St. Helena Island, off the coast of Georgia.*

White reaction

Although many white Southerners benefited from rations and medical care in the bureau's first two years, most white Southerners resented the bureau. They saw it as something imposed on them by the heavy-handed North. They attacked bureau officials and killed several agents. At the end of Reconstruction, whites succeeded in imposing discriminatory Black Codes across the South. These laws were intended to control freedmen's lives and restrict their freedom.

⟳ African Americans wait in line outside the office of the local Freedman's Bureau.

ASK YOURSELF

If Southerners thought the bureau had been forced on them, was there any chance it could have succeeded?

THE RIGHT ANSWER

?

What was the legacy of the Freedmen's Bureau in the development of the United States?

Before the Civil War, the federal government rarely got involved in Americans' lives. The Freedmen's Bureau broke new ground as a social agency that was actively involved in how individuals lived. It provided former slaves with a safety net and a welfare system. No welfare system had ever existed before—but it has existed ever since. The bureau also established a precedent for federal involvement in how each state ran its affairs. The amount of federal involvement in state business is an issue that continues to divide Americans today.

Legacy of the Civil War

The war was a watershed that changed the United States forever. It preserved the Union, which was its original stated aim. But it also abolished slavery and strengthened federal power.

The Civil War finally ended a debate that had continued since the Union formed in 1776 over whether states could choose to secede, or leave the Union. The Union is now accepted as unbreakable. Before the Civil War, Americans spoke of their nation as "these United States." After the war, it became "the United States."

◊ Civil War veterans meet on the Bull Run (Manassas) battlefield in 1881. Veterans would dominate politics for decades after the war.

Stronger federal powers

The Civil War changed the relationship between Americans and the federal government. Lincoln's administration introduced measures like the first income tax, which directly impacted individuals. There were similar laws in the South. Lincoln also set a precedent by using executive orders far more than his predecessors. The draft he introduced was used to raise soldiers until the end of the 20th century.

The Lincoln Memorial in Washington, D.C. For many Americans, Lincoln was the savior of the Union who determined both the outcome of the war and its legacy.

Slavery ends

Although ending slavery was not the original aim of the Lincoln administration, it became the war's defining action. Emancipation freed the potential of millions of former slaves and their descendants to contribute to the good of the nation. More than 180,000 black men eventually served in the Union military and helped to fight for their people's freedom.

Lincoln's most famous wartime executive order was his Emancipation Proclamation of January 1, 1863.

A new political system

The modern American two-party system emerged during the war. The Republican Party came to long-term power and remained the party of the North. The Democratic Party was the dominant party of the South. The Republicans were celebrated as the party that had freed the slaves.

ASK YOURSELF

Do you think the tolerant nature of many Americans can be seen as one of the legacies of the Civil War?

It was only in the 1930s that the Democratic Party became associated with the cause of the underprivileged.

In the aftermath of the war, three amendments were added to the U.S. Constitution. Southern states tried to avoid obeying them for the next century. In the 1950s and 1960s, civil rights activists used them to fight for equality.

The Thirteenth Amendment abolished slavery. The Fourteenth Amendment granted citizenship to anyone born in the United States. The Fifteenth gave the vote to African American men.

Industrial warfare

The Industrial Revolution played a key role in how the war was fought. Ironclad warships, submarines, aerial reconnaissance (balloons), and machine guns all made their first appearance. Trench warfare became common: it would be seen again in World War I (1914–1918). Railroads moved armies quickly, and the telegraph kept battle commanders in communication.

The effort in the North to mobilize

⟳ **The Capitol building in Washington, D.C., was half-built when war began. Lincoln decided to finish it as a symbol that the Union would survive.**

industrial production to meet wartime demands led to an increase in the size and scale of industrial organizations. "Bigness" would become a mark of postwar corporate America.

Cultural legacy

The Civil War still inspires novelists, poets, artists, and filmmakers. In the South, memories of the "Lost Cause"—a belief that the South had been betrayed by the North—permeated popular culture, as seen in the lasting popularity of movies like *Gone with the Wind*.

⊙ *Activists march for civil rights in the 1960s. The rights given a century before to African Americans had still not been truly realized.*

THE RIGHT ANSWER

?

If the Civil War had not ended slavery, what would its legacy have been?

The historian Barbara Fields said, "Without emancipation, the war was nothing but meaningless carnage." Freeing four million slaves changed the United States completely. Society slowly became more equal, although equality would not actually come until late in the 20th century. When African Americans became equal, it can be argued that the United States finally became a true democracy. Without the end of slavery, the United States would have remained a divided and feudal society, where a person was judged by the color of his or her skin.

Literature

The Civil War coincided with a boom period for American literature known as the American Renaissance. Later, a huge amount of literature was produced about the war and its impact.

UNCLE TOM'S CABIN.

🔊 *A poster advertising* Uncle Tom's Cabin. *The novel sold 300,000 copies in its first year and was quickly made into a popular play.*

The war itself is sometimes said to have been started by Harriet Beecher Stowe's bestselling novel, *Uncle Tom's Cabin*, written in 1852. It described the horrors of slavery and caused outrage in the North, where many people had little or no experience of slavery. It strengthened support for the abolitionist movement, which wanted to forbid slavery, and deepened the split between North and South.

Wartime songs and poems

An outburst of patriotism on both sides at the start of the war was reflected in songs and poems. The Union's anthem became "The Battle-Hymn of the Republic," while Confederates sang "Maryland, My Maryland" and "The Bonnie Blue Flag." The Quaker poet John Greenleaf Whittier wrote the pro-Union poem "Barbara Frietchie" in

1863. It tells the story of an old woman who waves her Union flag as General "Stonewall" Jackson and his Confederates ride through Frederick, Maryland. Barbara Frietchie was a real person, but the incident was probably made up.

Poets such as Whittier are largely forgotten now. Why not read one of his poems and see if you think that is fair?

Poetry of the North

Walt Whitman (1819–1892) was one of the most original poets of the 19th century. He is best known for *Leaves of Grass* (1855), but he also wrote two collections of poems during the war. They reflected his own experience as a volunteer nurse in military hospitals.

The other leading poet of the time was Emily Dickinson (1830–1886). Unlike Whitman, she had little direct involvement with the war. She wrote some 800 poems, although only seven were published in her lifetime, and none under her own name.

Few works were published during the Civil War, as both sides concentrated all their resources on essential services. Most of the writers who emerged after the war came from the North, because the South was culturally and economically shattered. Popular collections of poetry included H. H. Brownell's *War Lyrics* (1866), a book of

⟳ Sidney Lanier served as a Confederate soldier before becoming a famous writer.

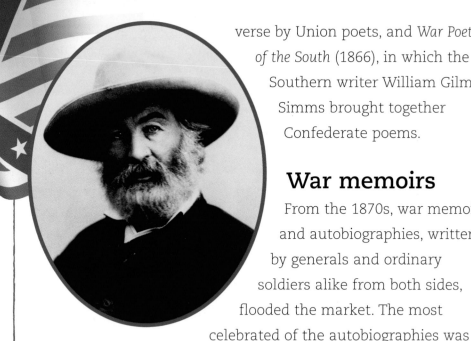

verse by Union poets, and *War Poetry of the South* (1866), in which the Southern writer William Gilmore Simms brought together Confederate poems.

War memoirs

From the 1870s, war memoirs and autobiographies, written by generals and ordinary soldiers alike from both sides, flooded the market. The most celebrated of the autobiographies was written by Ulysses S. Grant, the former Union general who became president in 1869. Grant barely completed his *Personal Memoirs* before his death in 1885. The book sold extremely well, earning his family $450,000 in only a short time.

In 1888, illustrated eyewitness accounts of the war from *Century* magazine were collected in four volumes entitled *Battles and Leaders of the Civil War*. Other popular accounts came from nurses or spies. The writer Louisa May Alcott (1832–1888) published *Hospital Sketches* (1863), a collection of letters she had written as a Civil War nurse in Washington, D.C.

Stories that took place in a certain part of the country were popular, especially if they were about the South. Thomas Nelson Page's stories about plantation life in Virginia were told in black

⌒ Walt Whitman served as a volunteer nurse to soldiers of both sides. His experiences inspired his collections Drum-Taps *(1865) and* Sequel to Drum-Taps *(1866).*

Alcott is best known for her semiautobiographical novel *Little Women* (1868), about four sisters growing up in the Civil War.

dialect. They described a chivalrous and idyllic South where black slaves were happy. The books were popular in both the North and the South.

Later works

Stephen Crane, born after the end of the conflict, wrote *The Red Badge of Courage* in 1895. It was notable for its realistic battle scenes. But the most famous literary work about the Civil War is Margaret Mitchell's only novel, *Gone with the Wind* (1936). This Pulitzer Prize–winning story of the Old South's destruction runs to 1,000 pages. It became the best-selling novel in U.S. history and was also a famous movie.

Why do you think such idealized books might have been so popular?

ASK YOURSELF

How much of what we know today about the Civil War comes from works of fiction or movies? Is that better or worse than learning about it from history?

THE RIGHT ANSWER

?

Harriet Beecher Stowe's *Uncle Tom's Cabin* has been said to have started the war. Why would that be?

Uncle Tom's Cabin told the story of Tom, a slave, and his treatment by three different masters whose behavior ranged from kind to cruel. The novel made a great impact because it showed how slavery brutalized both the slave and the master. When it was published in 1852, it gave many Northern readers a first introduction to the horrors of slavery, although critics called it propaganda. The book undoubtedly helped push the issue of slavery to the front of American politics. President Lincoln called Stowe "The little woman who wrote the book that caused this great war."

Lost Cause

The phrase "Lost Cause" refers to a set of beliefs adopted by Southerners after the war to explain how the Confederacy had lost. They saw the Old South as an idyll that had been taken from them.

T he historian Edward A. Pollard first used the phrase "Lost Cause" in 1866 to describe the Confederacy as a brave institution inevitably brought down by a cruel enemy. The term stood for the South's memory of what the Old South had been and what it had lost.

⟳ *This poem celebrating the Lost Cause, illustrated with images of Southern bank notes, was published soon after the war.*

The ideas of the myth

The Lost Cause myth argued that it was not slavery that caused the war, but the struggle for states' rights. Southerners were the true patriots, and secession was the only way for them to escape their Northern oppressors. They did not see slavery as an abuse of human rights. Instead, they saw the Old South as an ideal society where masters took care of contented slaves. Novels by writers such as Thomas N. Page reinforced this belief.

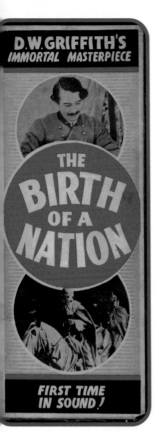

Another key part of the Lost Cause belief was that Confederate defeat was inevitable from the start of the war. The North's superior manpower and industrial strength meant it would inevitably win. But the Confederacy had the better leaders and soldiers. Confederate generals, such as Robert E. Lee and Thomas "Stonewall" Jackson, were treated like saints.

Reconstruction

The Lost Cause myth played a significant part in how the former Confederate states developed after the Civil War. It justified the existence of terrorist activities of racist organizations such as the Ku Klux Klan. For those who believed in the Lost Cause, the Klansmen were not motivated by race; they were fighting interfering Northerners and dangerous freed slaves. After federal troops left the South in 1877, the beliefs that underlay the Lost Cause helped create a racially segregated society that persisted into the middle of the 20th century. The rights of African Americans were gradually eroded in the last decades of the 19th century.

↩ *A poster of D. W. Griffith's epic 1915 movie* The Birth of a Nation. *The movie had many themes from the Lost Cause myth and idealized the Ku Klux Klan.*

Southerners had patriotic holidays, monuments, and organizations to honor all their dead soldiers, not just the leading generals.

ASK YOURSELF

If the North had stamped down on the Lost Cause, would Civil Rights have been better protected?

Coming together

At the end of the war, many Northerners saw the Southerners' refusal to accept defeat as arrogant. But over time, they began to admit that many Southerners had made sacrifices for their cause, no matter how misguided that cause had been. To help reconciliation and reunion, the heroism of the soldiers on both sides was emphasized more than the actual causes of the war.

The Lost Cause version of events became more acceptable as Northerners learned more about Southern life. Both Northerners and Southerners rushed to see D. W. Griffith's silent movie *The Birth*

By around 1900, commemorations were held across the nation as a means of bridging the gap between former enemies.

⊃ *This poster of Confederate generals and politicians was printed in 1896, some 30 years after the war, when the Lost Cause myth was at its height. Standing, left to right: Stonewall Jackson, Pierre G.T. Beauregard, and Robert E. Lee.*

of a Nation (1915). It portrayed Southern resistance to Reconstruction and the Ku Klux Klan in a positive way. Margaret Mitchell's bestselling novel *Gone with the Wind* (1936) was later turned into a hugely successful movie. The story line can in some ways be seen as another version of the Lost Cause myth, with its description of a somewhat idealized plantation life.

The civil rights struggle of the 1950s and 1960s was perhaps the last time the Lost Cause was evoked. Many people who objected to giving civil rights to African Americans justified their opposition in terms that recalled the Lost Cause myth.

↻ **Statues of Confederate soldiers, like Robert E. Lee, stand throughout the South.**

THE RIGHT ANSWER

?

Who was most likely to have believed in the myth of the Lost Cause?

The Lost Cause said that slavery was not the problem that had caused the Civil War. That appealed mainly to Southerners. Not everyone in the South owned slaves, but everyone benefited from slavery. The whole economy was based on free labor. The Lost Cause was attractive because it used Southerners' fabled manners to show how civilized the South was. This part of the myth also appealed to Northerners, as it seemed to reflect a simpler time in American history. Many Northerners also agreed with the myth's belief that whites were naturally superior to blacks.

Memorials and Souvenirs

Before the war was even over, honoring the dead started to become more formal and ceremonial.

🔊 *This relief showing Union soldiers is on the Ulysses S. Grant memorial near the Capitol in Washington, D.C.*

Acts of remembrance began casually. After battles, soldiers and local people searched the ground for bullets or buttons to act as souvenirs. But before the war had ended, the process was growing more formal. In 1864, at Manassas, Virginia, Union officers erected a monument to their fellows who had died on the battlefield. In the South, meanwhile, women's groups held ceremonies to put flowers on the graves of Confederate dead. First observed at the end of May 1868, when the spring flowers were at their best, the practice became Memorial Day.

Building memorials

For the first decades after the war, Southerners put most of their monuments in cemeteries. From about 1885, veterans' groups and state-level monument committees in both the North and South increasingly placed memorials on the battlefields. Gettysburg, Pennsylvania, was the site of the war's largest battle and one of the most significant. It became a focal point of remembrance for both sides.

In the South, monument unveiling days were a focus for resistance to Republican policies. Nearly 50,000 people came to Richmond, Virginia, on October 26, 1875. They watched the unveiling of a new monument to General Thomas "Stonewall" Jackson—and listened to speeches calling for the overthrow of Reconstruction.

The battlefield at Gettysburg is home to many different types of monument: obelisks, large amphitheaters, and statues of soldiers.

A federal interest

In the 1870s, Union general Daniel Sickles became the head of the New York State Monuments Commission. He and others prevented Confederate veterans' organizations from building monuments to the Southern dead. Even today, most Confederate memorials tend to be placed in one area of a battlefield. They are often placed around the start line of the attacks on the second or third day of battle.

From the 1880s, the U.S. government started to turn

⏬ *The African American Civil War Monument, commemorating black Americans who served in the Union army and navy, was created in Washington, D.C., in 1997.*

battlefields into permanent memorials. They were designated national battlefields or national historical parks and protected accordingly.

Capital memorials

Both of the Civil War capitals, Washington, D.C., and Richmond, Virginia, contain many reminders of their Civil War past. Washington, D.C., has more monuments dedicated to the conflict than to any other event in the nation's history. These include more equestrian statues than in any other city in the United States. At one end of the National Mall in the heart of Washington, D.C., is the Lincoln Memorial. The marble statue shows a seated figure of Abraham Lincoln, surrounded by the texts of his wartime speeches and by a mural that shows the emancipation of the slaves. Hollywood Cemetery in Richmond, Virginia, has many memorials dedicated to Confederate generals as well as thousands of graves of ordinary soldiers. On the edge of downtown Richmond is Monument Avenue, a broad thoroughfare with memorials dedicated to the most famous Confederate generals from Virginia.

The house in Appomattox where the surrender was signed was stripped of souvenirs by Union soldiers.

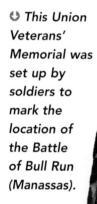

◑ *This Union Veterans' Memorial was set up by soldiers to mark the location of the Battle of Bull Run (Manassas).*

Other reminders

THE SOLDIER'S MEMORIAL.

Many small towns across America, particularly in the South, have memorials to Civil War soldiers. These monuments commemorate the local men who went to war. At the University of North Carolina, for example, a statue known as "Silent Sam" remembers the students who fought in the conflict. Such statues serve to remind modern Americans on a daily basis about the cost of war.

C The Soldier's Memorial is a print created in 1863; it shows a woman grieving beside a soldier's tomb.

ASK YOURSELF

Have you noticed a memorial where you live? Does it remind you about the loss of life in the Civil War and in wars being fought today?

THE RIGHT ANSWER

?

Memorials to the Civil War are common across the country. Do they still have a purpose?

The Civil War was the single most cataclysmic event in American national history. It divided the nation in a way that had not been seen before or since. At its heart was the question of how humans should treat other humans. The emancipation of the slaves showed a commitment to equality, even if true equality remained a long way off. The memorials of the war are a reminder of the many personal sacrifices that went into that commitment. They are also reminders of the sacrifices of today's military and of the capacity of former enemies to achieve reconciliation.

Movies

Movies with a Civil War setting have always been popular. The best of them entertain and inform new audiences, but the worst of them are biased and give an unbalanced view of the war.

S ince the start of the movie industry, the Civil War has provided material for many filmmakers. The earliest films about the conflict included *Granddad* (1913), *The Drummer of the 8th* (1913), and *The Coward* (1915). These early movies highlighted the horrors and upheaval of war.

☟ **Gone with the Wind** *starred Clark Gable and Vivien Leigh in one of the greatest love stories in movies.*

The Birth of a Nation

D. W. Griffith made his epic movie *The Birth of a Nation* in 1915. It tells the story of two families during the Civil War, one in the North and the other in the South. The movie was a huge box-office hit, but it was later criticized for being racist: it ends with a Ku Klux Klan procession.

Another famous silent movie about the war was *The General* (1926). The comedy starred Buster Keaton as an unlucky train engineer whose locomotive is stolen by Union men.

In a scene from the 1951 movie The Red Badge of Courage, *young boys who have been playing soldiers hide in the woods as a real battle begins.*

Gone with the Wind

Probably the best-known of all Civil War movies is *Gone with the Wind* (1939). The movie tells the story of a pampered Southern belle, Scarlett O'Hara (Vivien Leigh), and her love–hate relationship with blockade-runner Rhett Butler (Clark Gable). The movie contains spectacular historical scenes, including the burning of Atlanta. But its romantic view of the Old South and slavery led to it, too, being accused of racism.

Gone with the Wind was based on the best-selling novel by Margaret Mitchell. It covers the period from before the war to the end of Reconstruction.

Western directors

Many directors who made Westerns also made movies based on events from the Civil War. These included John Ford, who made *The Horse Soldiers* in 1959. The famous Western star John Wayne

ASK YOURSELF

Do you think people believe what they see in a movie more than what they read in a novel?

⊃ *Clint Eastwood and Geraldine Page star in* The Beguiled *(1971). It is about a wounded Union soldier who is nursed in a Confederate girls' school.*

TV miniseries about the Civil War include *The Blue and the Gray* (1982) and the romance *North and South* (1985).

played a Union cavalryman on a dangerous mission. In 1976, the actor Clint Eastwood directed and starred in *The Outlaw Josey Wales*. He played a Missouri farmer who became an outlaw after Union guerrillas killed his wife and child.

In recent decades, television has made factual and nonfactual miniseries about the Civil War, such as the acclaimed *Roots* (1977). Longer than movies, such series had more time to examine the origins and impact of the war. In 1990, Ken Burns released *The Civil War*, still considered the best documentary series made about the war.

The black soldier in movies

Glory (1989) was about a black regiment, the 54th Massachusetts. The movie was based on a real regiment. Many of its scenes were fictional, but it also re-created historical events such as the 54th's courageous but doomed attack on Fort Wagner in Charleston Harbor in 1863.

> The 54th Massachusetts was made up of black volunteers commanded by a white officer.

Gettysburg

Gettysburg (1993) was filmed on the site of the 1863 battle. To make it as authentic as possible, thousands of extras were used. In 2003, the film's writer-director Ronald F. Maxwell made a prequel, *Gods and Generals*, about the war's first two years.

> **ASK YOURSELF**
>
> Why do you think people are still making movies about the Civil War? Isn't it all too long ago now?

THE RIGHT ANSWER

?

Movies about the Civil War have always been popular. Are they a good way of learning about the past?

We tend to learn about history from first-hand accounts, books, or photographs, or perhaps by visiting historical sites or museums. Movies often present the past in an entertaining way, so that we can "learn" about history without making much effort. Many movies are quite authentic, but they can never tell the whole story. And movie directors sometimes sacrifice accuracy for the sake of their story. So although movies are a way to start learning about the past, books and other accounts can often give more detailed and more balanced information.

National Cemeteries

There are 120 national cemeteries across the country that serve as resting places for the war dead. The Union first purchased land to build cemeteries for their dead in July 1862.

🎧 *A mourner visits a Civil War cemetery in Alexandria, Virginia.*

W hen the Civil War started, both sides believed it would be a short conflict with little loss of life. The battles of spring and summer 1862, such as Shiloh and the Seven Days' Battles, proved that that was not to be the case. The huge loss of life led to a desperate need for burial grounds for dead soldiers. On July 17, 1862, Congress authorized President Abraham Lincoln to buy land to be turned into national cemeteries.

COMMENT

More than 4,000 Union dead from Antietam were buried in a cemetery near the battlefield.

Burying the dead

The 1862 act set up 14 Union cemeteries. They were close to the scenes of battles to make it easier to bury the dead. After the Battle of Gettysburg, Lincoln dedicated a new cemetery next to the battlefield on November 19, 1863, and gave his famous Gettysburg Address.

There were no dedicated war cemeteries in the South. Confederate soldiers were buried where they fell or in public cemeteries or family plots. As the death toll climbed late in the war, however, the Confederate government took over private land for military burials.

After the war

After the end of the war, the U.S. government set up a national cemetery system. It undertook to remove Union dead buried on the battlefields for burial in new cemeteries. Burial teams scoured the South to locate the remains of Union soldiers buried where they fell. By 1870, nearly 300,000 Union dead had been reburied in 73 cemeteries. Half of the soldiers were unidentified.

Respecting the bodies of the fallen is an important part of war. The Union understood this from the start, unlike the Confederates.

ASK YOURSELF

Do you think people who die fighting for the country deserve a proper funeral and grave?

↻ *Southern women look after soldiers' graves in Charleston, South Carolina, in 1903.*

Many Southerners were angered that no equivalent system existed to rebury the Confederate dead. Volunteers formed the Ladies' Memorial Association to clean and decorate Confederate graves. People who owned plots in public cemeteries, such as Oakwood and Hollywood in Richmond, Virginia, often donated their plots for military burials.

In 1866, the *Richmond Examiner* complained, "The unfortunate Confederate soldier lies where he met his death."

Graves for veterans

In 1873, a new law was passed to allow all honorably discharged veterans to be buried in national cemeteries. Pre–Civil War military dead

➲ *Arlington Cemetery in Virginia is sited on land that once belonged to the wife of Confederate general Robert E. Lee. The Union buried 5,000 Union dead there between May 1864 and the end of the war.*

who had died in the American Revolution (1775–1783) or in the War of 1812 were formally reinterred in the cemeteries. Today, the National Cemetery Administration runs 120 national cemeteries in 39 states and in Puerto Rico, covering 14,000 acres (5,600 ha) of federal land.

Arlington Cemetery in Virginia, the country's most important military cemetery, was created from land that once belonged to the wife of Confederate general Robert E. Lee. Lee spent time there as a young man. In 1864, it was turned into a resting place for Union war dead.

Arlington Cemetery now covers 624 acres (253 ha) and has more than 300,000 graves.

THE RIGHT ANSWER

?

Why did people in the South have fewer official burials for the Civil War dead?

Southerners considered themselves to be more refined and better mannered than their Northern neighbors. They considered the Southern way of life far more "civilized" than that in the North. But as the war went on and the South grew more impoverished, it could not continue its elegant way of life. This was seen clearly in how it treated its war dead. Unlike the North, which set up a federal, centralized system of burial, the Southern system was on a far more ad-hoc basis. The Confederates relied on friends and families to bury their dead.

Reconstruction

The Reconstruction period (1865–1877) saw the 11 Confederate states rejoin the Union. Congress hoped to reshape the South, but Southerners resented what they saw as outside interference.

COMMENT

The South was under effective military occupation until 1877, when the last federal troops left.

T he end of the war in April 1865 left great uncertainty about the future of the defeated Confederate states and what would happen to former slaves now they had been emancipated.

Presidential intentions

In 1863, with the end of the war far off, President Abraham Lincoln began the job of reconstructing Confederate territory under Union occupation. Despite opposition, Lincoln pushed through his plan, and governments were formed in Louisiana, Arkansas, Tennessee, and Virginia. Lincoln preferred an approach that did not punish the South. In March 1865, a month before the war ended and his death, he declared his intention to rebuild the nation "with malice toward none, with charity for all." Lincoln was assassinated on April 14. That left his successor,

⟳ *Freedmen gather outside a schoolroom in the South during Reconstruction.*

Andrew Johnson, to take charge of the transition. Although he was a staunch Unionist, Johnson was also a Southerner who had little interest in the fate of African Americans.

Reconstruction

Between April and December 1865, civil government was restored in all the former Confederate states, with the exception of Texas. The new state governments immediately passed the Black Codes, laws that restricted the ability of freedmen to own land and work as free laborers, and denied them political rights. Congress then passed the Civil Rights Act in April 1866 to protect the freedmen from the Black Codes.

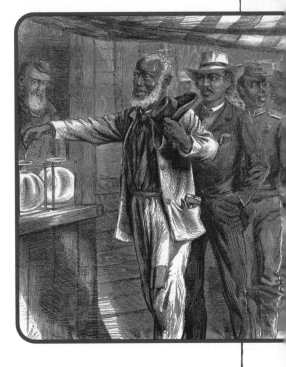

🎧 **African Americans voting in 1867 for the first time in the South as shown in an Alfred Waud drawing.**

The New South

In 1867, Congress passed the Reconstruction Acts. Under their terms, six states (Arkansas, North Carolina, South Carolina, Louisiana, Alabama, and Florida) were readmitted to the Union in 1868. The four remaining states—Virginia, Texas, Mississippi, and Georgia—rejoined in 1870.

Reconstruction was widely opposed in the South, in part because of widespread hatred of the Republican Party. But the votes of former

ASK YOURSELF

Do you think African Americans would have been allowed to vote without federal soldiers to back their rights?

slaves meant the Republicans now also had electoral success in the South. Republican success was enforced by military power: the South was under occupation by federal troops. Democrats accused the Republicans of taking control through violence.

Equal rights

For a brief time, many African Americans voted; some entered politics and even became senators. White Southerners reacted violently. Groups such as the Ku Klux Klan used terrorism to stop blacks from voting. Many of their objections were based on racism, but Southerners also resented being turned into "Yankees." They saw the South as being controlled by "carpetbaggers"—Northerners

A Northern cartoon of 1865 shows two Southern women snubbing a Union soldier in a Richmond street.

who went South after the war in search of economic opportunities—and their Southern allies, the "scalawags."

Read more about the carpetbaggers and scalawags on pages 6-9.

Reconstruction ends

Northern interest in racial equality in the South eventually began to fade. The Southerner intimidation of black voters was so successful that Democrats soon controlled all but three Southern states. The next president, Ulysses S. Grant, tried to uphold the rights of Southern blacks. After Grant left office, however, the disputed presidential election of 1876 brought the end of Reconstruction.

ASK YOURSELF

The South was forced to take on many changes very quickly. Would it have been better to go slowly, even if it took longer to get more equal rights?

THE RIGHT ANSWER

?

Considering the circumstances, was it remarkable that Reconstruction lasted as long as it did?

Reconstruction lasted from 1865 to 1877. Even before the war ended, President Lincoln knew that reincorporating the 11 Confederate states would be difficult. Radicals in the North wanted the South to be given stricter terms for rejoining. In the South, there was massive opposition to the freeing of slaves. This allowed organizations like the Ku Klux Klan to rise and dominate Southern politics. Between these two extremes, Congress and the president had to find a middle way that was acceptable to both sides. That they managed to reincorporate the South was an achievement.

Glossary

amendment: A new clause that is added to the U.S. Constitution to change or clarify its original terms.

Black Codes: A series of laws introduced in the South to limit the rights of African Americans.

carpetbagger: A Northern Republican who moved to the South after the war.

contracts: Legal agreements about property sales or terms of employment.

Emancipation: The abolition of slavery.

executive orders: Laws that are made by the president alone, rather than by Congress.

federal: Related to the national government based in Washington, D.C.

freedmen: The name given to slaves who had been liberated during and after the war.

guerrillas: Irregular soldiers who fought by methods such as ambushes and raids.

idyllic: An idealized view of a perfect lifestyle.

infrastructure: The physical structure that keeps a country running, such as roads.

Ku Klux Klan: An organization set up in the South to terrorize black Americans.

propaganda: Information that persuades people to support a particular point of view.

Reconstruction: The name given to the period from 1865 to 1876 when federal soldiers enforced government laws in the South.

reconciliation: The process of making former enemies become more friendly.

scalawag: A Southerner who supported the Republicans during Reconstruction.

plantations: Large agricultural estates used in the South to grow crops such as cotton.

welfare: A system of benefits and other state support for the poor or disadvantaged.

Further reading

Bozonelis, Helen Kontras. *200 Years with Abraham Lincoln: One Man's Life and Legacy*. Enslow Publications, 2008.

Flanagan, Timothy. *Reconstruction: A Primary Source History of the Struggle to United the North and South After the Civil War* (Primary Sources in American History). Rosen Publishing Group, 2004.

Greene, Meg. *Rest in Peace: A History of American Cemeteries* (People's History). Twenty-First Century Books, 2007.

Hankins, Chelsey. *The Lincoln Memorial* (Symbols of American Freedom). Chelsea House Publications, 2009.

McNeese, Tim. *Reconstruction: Life After the Civil War* (Civil War: A Nation Divided). Chelsea House Publishers, 2009.

Pierce, Alan. *Reconstruction* (American Moments). Abdo Publishing Company, 2005.

Stanchak, John E. *Civil War* (DK Eyewitness Books). DK Publishing, 2011.

Stroud, Bettye, and Virginia Schomp. *The Reconstruction Era* (Drama of African–American History). Benchmark Books, 2006.

Websites

PBS site on Reconstruction: The Second Civil War.
http//www.pbs.org/wgbh/amex/reconstruction/

Smithsonian Institution page with resources on the Civil War.
http//www.civilwar.si.edu

A site supporting the PBS film *The Civil War*, directed by Ken Burns.
http//www.pbs.org/civilwar

Library of Congress guide to Reconstruction from the African-American Odyssey exhibit, with primary sources.
http://memory.loc.gov/ammem/aaohtml/exhibit/aopart5.html

Index